Kingdom Parables

Written by Christopher A. Lane
With Illustrations by Sharon Dahl

VICTOR BOOKS

A DIVISION OF SCRIPTURE PRESS PUBLICATIONS INC.
USA CANADA ENGLAND

Cover design: Paul Higdon

3 4 5 6 7 8 9 10 Printing/Year 98 97 96 95

Published by Victor Books/SP Publications, Inc., Wheaton, Illinois.
All rights reserved. Printed in the United States of America.
These revised stories were originally individually published as *Kidderminister Kingdom Tales* by Christopher Lane and Sharon Dahl.

Contents

With thanks to Gordon, the love of my life,
and to Sam and Syd — my inspiration.

— S.D.

To Micah and Christopher
My little motivators
My daunting challenges
My sons

— C.L.

Sir Humphrey's Honeystands

The Unmerciful Servant
Matthew 18:21-35

There was once a bear who lived in a beautiful house deep in the forest. His name was Humphrey and he was very wealthy. In fact, he had so much money that he was a true millionbear. The woodland creatures considered him a royal animal, of sorts, and called him Sir Humphrey.

Humphrey had made his fortune in honey. After discovering an enormous beehive, he opened honeystands throughout the forest. Since he now had many servants to attend to his business, Humphrey spent his days relaxing in his spacious manor.

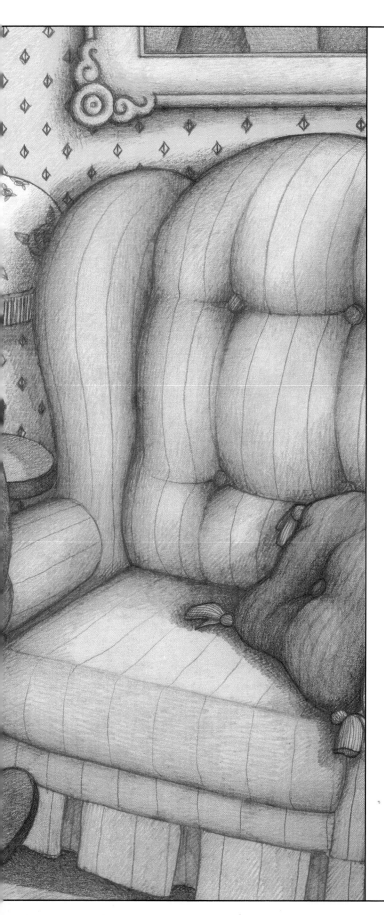

It came about one day that Edward, the bookkeeping beaver, was in Sir Humphrey's study checking the honey records.

"Oh, my," Edward said, "all of your honeystands are doing quite well, Sir Humphrey. But there seems to be a slight problem. One of your servants has — um — 'borrowed' several jars of honey and failed to return them or pay for them."

"How many jars?" Humphrey asked.

"According to these figures," Edward said, "he owes you . . . 100."

"100 jars!" Humphrey shouted. "What on earth could anyone do with 100 jars of honey?"

"I have no idea," Edward said, shaking his head. "But I certainly advise you to find out."

"Reginald!" Sir Humphrey roared.

Moments later a regal-looking hound appeared. "You rang, Sir?"

"Yes, Reginald, please summon—" Sir Humphrey paused. "Ed, what was the name of that servant?"

The beaver flipped through his papers. "It is Mr. Freddie the Fox."

"Freddie the Fox? Why, he is my most trusted servant," Sir Humphrey said in amazement. "Reginald, have Mr. Fox brought to me at once."

"Very good Sir," the sleepy-eyed butler said. "Will there be anything else, Sir? A cup of tea before your nap, perhaps?"

"No, Reginald," Humphrey sighed. "I am too upset for my tea or my nap today."

Later that afternoon, there was a knock at the door of Sir Humphrey's study. "Come in," he said in a deep voice.

The butler opened the door. "A Mr. Fox to see you, sir."

"Send him in. And have Ed my bookkeeper come in as well."

"Say, Sir Humphrey," Freddie said brightly as he and the beaver entered the study. "You gonna open another honeystand? I was thinkin' 'bout a place over by. . . ."

"That's not why I've asked you here, Freddie," Sir Humphrey interrupted. "Ed, tell Mr. Fox what you have found."

"According to these records, Mr. Fox, you owe Sir Humphrey 100 jars of honey."

"How do you explain this debt?" Humphrey asked, leaning toward the fox. "Did you take 100 jars?"

"I . . . ah . . ." Freddie stuttered. "Yeah, I guess so."

"What happened to it?" Sir Humphrey asked.

"I took some home to my family," Freddie explained. "You remember my family . . ." He pulled out a wallet filled with pictures.

"They couldn't possibly eat that much honey!" Humphrey bellowed.

"Well . . . no, we didn't eat it all," his voice sank to a whisper. "I kind of took some outside the forest and sold it."

"Where is the money, Freddie?"

"I sort of lost it. I have this weakness for the ponies. Thought I could make a little easy money."

"Gambling is never easy money, Mr. Fox," Edward said sternly. "Especially when you are using someone else's."

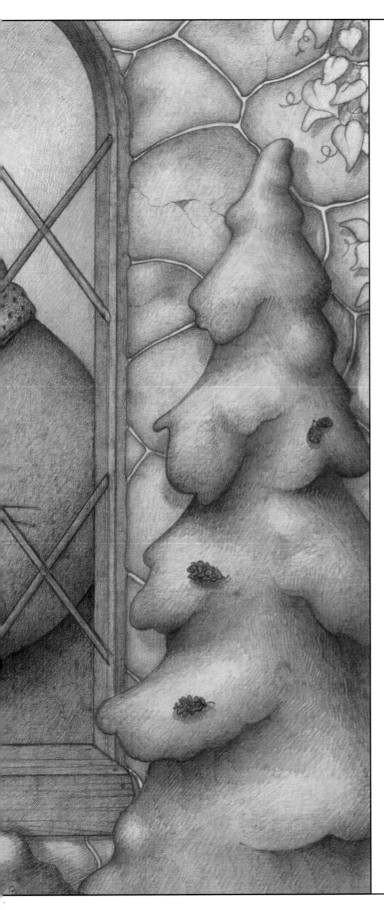

"You stole my honey, sold it, and gambled away the profits?" Humphrey asked.

The fox nodded. "But I'll pay you back."

"Yes, you will," Humphrey said. "Immediately!"

"But, sir," Freddie pleaded, "you can't mean that. How will we live? Oh, please, please, just give me some time. I'll pay back every single jar. Please, sir...."

"Oh, get up," Sir Humphrey said. "I should have you thrown into jail, but I can see that you are sorry for what you did. I forgive you."

"Oh, thank you, Sir!" Freddie cried. "I'll start paying you back as soon as—"

"You could never repay it all," the wealthy bear said, shaking his head. "Ed, strike out his debt."

"Oh, thank you, Sir, thank you," the overjoyed fox said.

"Now back to work with you," Sir Humphrey grumbled, "you crazy fox."

Later that same day, an elderly mole named Barnabas approached one of Sir Humphrey's honeystands. He was a poor animal who could only afford to buy small amounts of honey. This time the mole had no money at all, yet he was quite hungry.

"Why, hello there, Barnabas," the rabbit clerk said cheerily when she noticed him. "What can I do for you?"

"I—I was wondering, Mrs. Rabbit," he said slowly, "if I might have a bit of honey?"

"Of course," she said. Lowering her voice she added, "I'll put it on your bill."

"Why, thank you," the mole replied.

Mrs. Rabbit hopped over to the bin, dipped a generous cupful of honey, marked it in her receipt book, and then handed the cup to the waiting mole.

Just then Freddie the Fox arrived to make sure that business was running smoothly.

"Get me today's records, Mrs. Rabbit," Freddie ordered. "Hop, hop!"

Mrs. Rabbit scurried to gather the needed papers. "Here you are, Sir."

The fox looked them over. "Very well," he grunted. "I'll be back tomorrow."

Freddie turned to leave and walked right into Barnabas.

"Excuse me, Sir," the mole said as honey spilled onto the ground.

"You old fool!" Freddie hissed, wiping honey from his coat. Suddenly Freddie recognized him. "Hey, aren't you Barnabas?"

"Yes, Sir," the mole said, nodding politely.

Freddie shuffled through the records again. "Barnabas . . . Barnabas . . . Aha! According to this, you owe me for one cup of honey."

"Yes, I know, Sir, but —"

"No 'buts' about it." Freddie grabbed the elderly mole by the coat. "Pay up!"

"Mr. Fox!" Mrs. Rabbit protested. "Please don't shake him."

"You've gotta pay up right now, Barny ol' buddy," the fox continued. "Gimme this coat, and that cane, and let me have your hat."

"Please, Mr. Fox. Be patient," Barnabas begged, falling to his knees. "I promise to pay you back."

"Police!" Freddie yelled. "Police! This man won't pay his bill!"

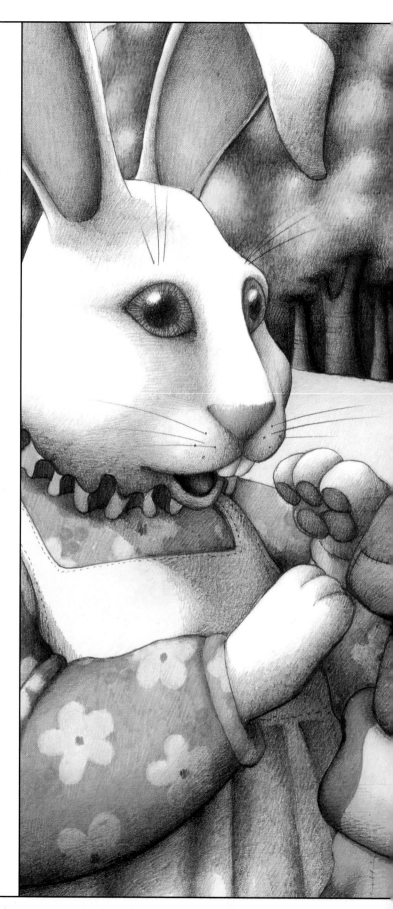

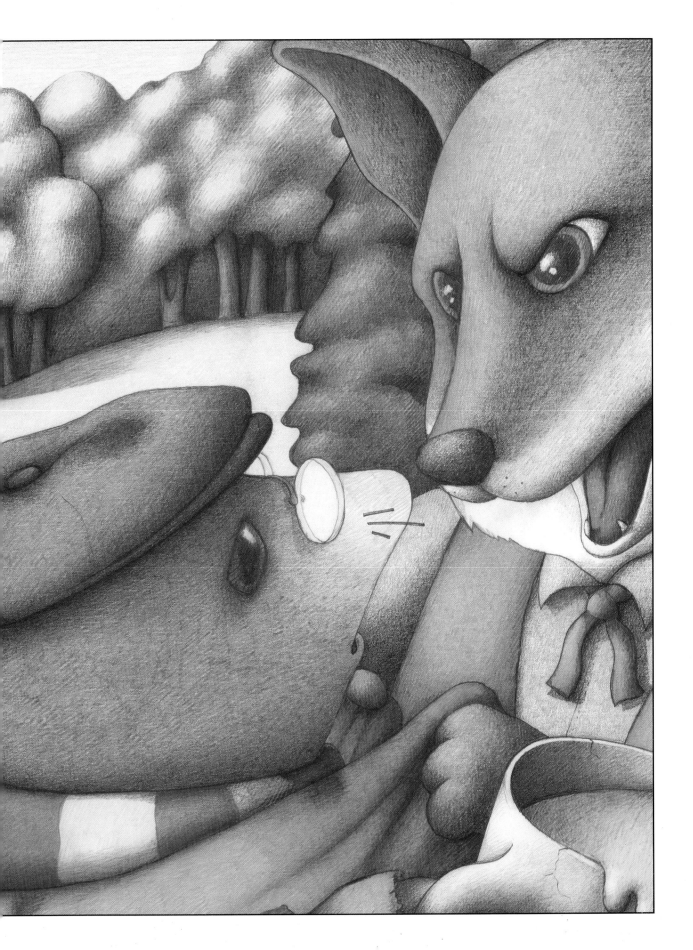

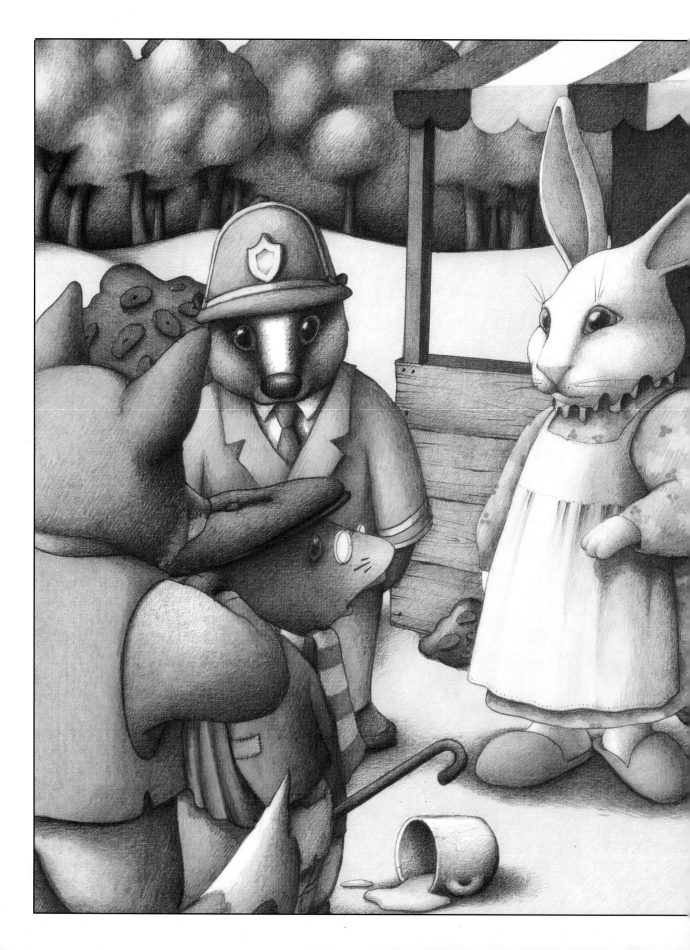

A few moments later, two badgers arrived from the nearby police station.

"What seems to be the problem here?" one of them asked.

"This bum won't pay his bill," Freddie said.

"Well, Sir, what do you have to say for yourself?" the second badger asked.

"I have no money," Barnabas answered, hanging his head.

"Sorry, fella," the first badger said, "we're gonna have to take you in."

Mrs. Rabbit began to cry as the two officers led Barnabas away toward the jail. But Freddie simply strolled off down the opposite path, humming a happy tune.

It didn't take Mrs. Rabbit long to realize that she simply had to do something to help Barnabas. And that something was to visit Sir Humphrey.

She was hopping up and down and had tears in her eyes by the time Reginald ushered her into the wealthy bear's study. "Oh, Sir Humphrey, it was terrible! That Freddie is so cruel." And she told him what had happened.

"Why that ungrateful little fox!" Sir Humphrey growled. "Reginald!"

"Yes, Sir," the butler replied, entering the parlor.

"Have Freddie the Fox summoned at once!"

When Freddie the Fox arrived, he strutted into the study without waiting for Reginald to announce him.

"Say, Sir H. What's up? Got a problem that old Freddie can help iron out?"

"Be quiet. You . . ." Sir Humphrey pointed, ". . . you worthless servant!"

"Huh?"

"First you steal from me. Then you have a respectable customer thrown into prison."

"You mean that Barnabas character? He's a bum, Sir H. I turned him over to the police."

"You should have forgiven him."

"Hey, he owed me!" Freddie objected.

"If you cannot forgive this small debt, then neither will I forgive you. Reginald!" Sir Humphrey roared. "Call the police!"

"What are you doing?" Freddie screeched.

"Sir," the butler said, "your other guests have arrived."

"Very good," Sir Humphrey smiled. "Show them in."

Freddie's eyes got big when he saw Barnabas the mole and Mrs. Rabbit walk in.

"They are here at my request," Sir Humphrey explained. "Mr. Barnabas will soon be managing one of my honeystands. And Mrs. Rabbit will be taking your job as chief over all my honeystand operations."

"What about me?" Freddie asked. "What am I going to do?"

"You, Mr. Fox, are going to jail," Sir Humphrey said flatly. "And there you will stay until you pay back every last jar of honey."

"You can't do this!" Freddie protested.

Reginald opened the door and the police officers stepped in.

"Come along, Mr. Fox," one of the officers said, grabbing Freddie by the scruff of his neck. And the two badgers carried him out the door.

Sir Humphrey waited until the door was closed. "Now, Mrs. Rabbit and Mr. Barnabas, we have things to discuss. As you know, selling honey can be sticky business. . . ."

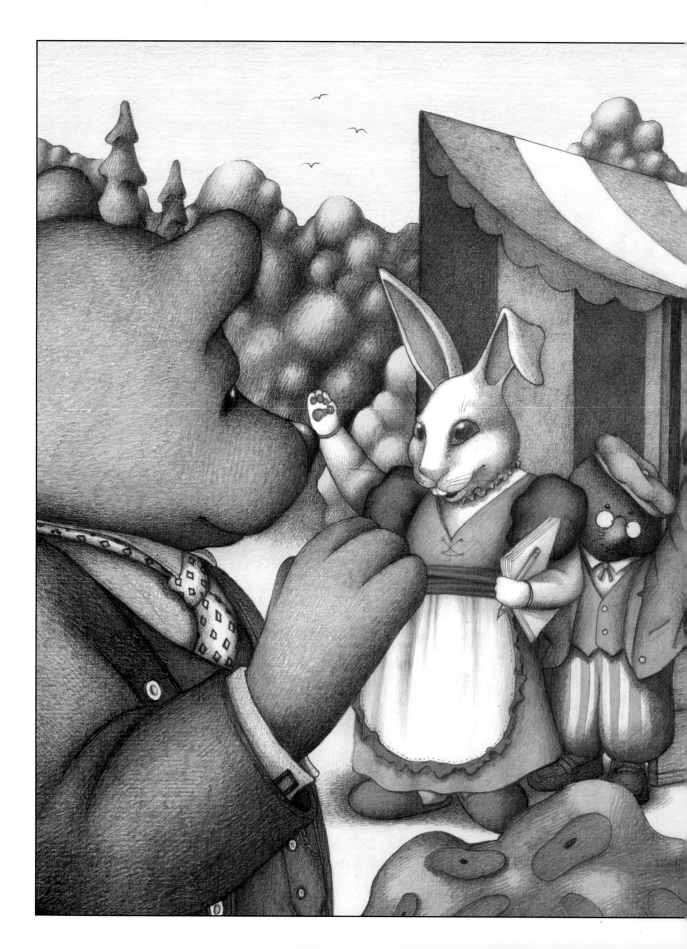

And so Sir Humphrey entrusted his honeystands to Mrs. Rabbit and Barnabas the mole. With these two faithful servants handling his affairs, Sir Humphrey was free to spend his days lounging in his spacious manor.

As for Freddie the Fox, he became known as the "fox who wouldn't forgive." He remains in jail to this day, still paying back his debt to Sir Humphrey. He now has only 95 and one half jars of honey to go.

You can read a story like this in the Bible. Jesus told it in Matthew 18:21-35:

Then Peter came to Jesus and asked, "Lord, how many times shall I forgive my brother when he sins against me?"

Jesus answered, "The kingdom of heaven is like a king who wanted to settle accounts with his servants. As he began the settlement, a man who owed him ten thousand talents [millions of dollars] was brought to him. Since he was not able to pay, the master ordered that he and his wife and his children and all that he had be sold to repay the debt.

"The servant fell on his knees before him. 'Be patient with me,' he begged, 'and I will pay you back everything.' The servant's master took pity on him, canceled the debt, and let him go.

"But when that servant went out, he found one of his fellow servants who owed him a hundred denarii [a few dollars]. He grabbed him and began to choke him. 'Pay back what you owe me!' he demanded.

"His fellow servant fell to his knees and begged him, 'Be patient with me, and I will pay you back.'

"But he refused. Instead, he went off and had the man thrown into prison until he could pay the debt. When the other servants saw what had happened, they were greatly distressed and went and told their master everything that had happened.

"Then the master called the servant in. 'You wicked servant,' he said, 'I canceled all that debt of yours because you begged me to. Shouldn't you have had mercy on your fellow servant just as I had on you?' In anger his master turned him over to the jailers to be tortured, until he should pay back all he owed.

"This is how my heavenly Father will treat each of you unless you forgive your brother from your heart."

Nicholas and His Neighbors

The Good Samaritan
Luke 10:25-37

There was once a village called Pupland nestled in a beautiful green valley. Down its quaint cobblestone streets trotted every size, shape, and color of dog imaginable.

One resident, however, stood out from all the rest. His name was Nicholas, and he looked unlike any of the dogs in all of Pupland.

You see, Nicholas was a cat.

Nicholas so loved farming that he had purchased one of the fields outside the village. He enjoyed tilling the ground and planting seeds, and he did not at all mind having dogs for neighbors.

But having a cat for a neighbor did bother the citizens of Pupland. In their opinion, he just didn't fit in.

One dog particularly disliked Nicholas. His name was Ned, and he was the sheriff of Pupland.

Ned first noticed Nicholas on a quiet Friday afternoon. Ned was relaxing in the town square when he saw a farmer pushing a cart full of vegetables.

As the cart approached, Ned suddenly realized that the farmer was not a dog, but a cat. Leaping to his feet, he rushed to block Nicholas' path. "Where do you think you're going, Cat?" Ned growled.

"I've brought my vegetables to sell to the townsdogs," Nicholas replied happily.

"Pack 'em up and go back to your cat friends!" Ned ordered.

"But I thought this was a free town where both dogs and cats could do business."

Nicholas was right. There was no law against cats selling their goods in Pupland.

Ned growled again and stepped aside. "Go ahead and peddle your goods," he called after him. "No dog will buy vegetables from a cat!"

At the end of each week, it was the same story. Nicholas would bring his produce to market and Ned would pester him.

Early one summer morning, Nicholas was out tilling the soil in his field. He felt especially happy because he was about to go to a family reunion in Pussywillow.

On this day, Ned the Sheriff was also going on a trip. He was on his way to the "Be Mean to Cats Association" meeting in nearby Poochville. Ned was the treasurer of the group and was in charge of bringing the piggy bank.

As he walked along, Ned noticed Nicholas' farm. Spying the cat working in his field, Ned suddenly had an idea.

Setting aside his bag and piggy bank, he snuck up behind Nicholas and let out a bellowing bark.

Nicholas was so startled that he dropped his rake and jumped high into the air, losing his hat and landing in a nearby stack of hay.

"Good morning, Mr. Nicholas!" Ned chuckled. "Rather jumpy today, aren't we?"

With a big grin on his face, Ned continued on his way toward Poochville.

Nicholas was upset, but not for long. He soon remembered his family reunion and cheered right up. When his chores were done, he changed into his best overalls and donned a new bandana. Loading his cart with vegetables to share with his family, he began his journey.

Upon reaching the Poochville Highway, he noticed a sign. "Beware of Thieves," he read. "Hmm. I certainly hope there are no thieves out today."

Now it just so happened that a pack of wild dogs was indeed planning an ambush. Hidden behind a row of thick bushes, these ruffians were waiting to take advantage of an unwary traveler.

"Nothing," Sid said, peering through his binoculars. "Hold it — here comes someone." It was a dog carrying a bag and a piggy bank.

"Someone's coming?" Mugsy yelped, bouncing up and down.

"Knock it off, Mugsy!" Bruno barked, swiping at Mugsy with his large paw.

"Missed me, you big lug!" Mugsy teased.

"Cut the chatter!" Sid ordered. "You guys know the routine. Let's do it."

And they all took their places.

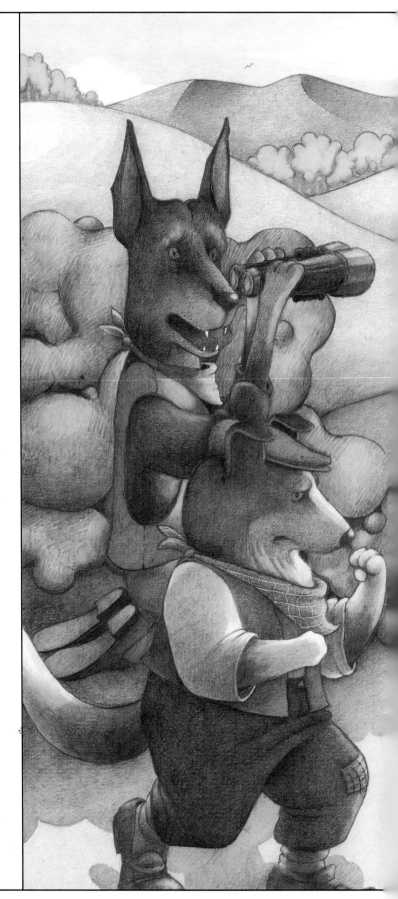

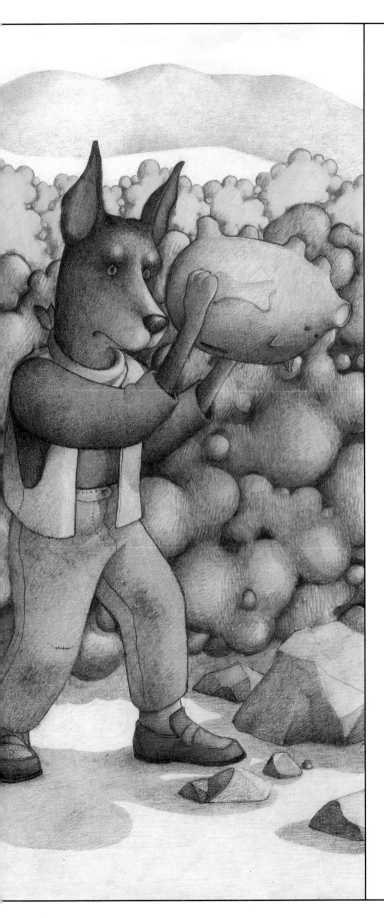

"Excuse me, Sir," Mugsy whined pitifully as he emerged from the bushes. "Can you spare a small biscuit for a hungry dog?"

"I guess," Ned replied, rummaging through his suitcase.

But before Ned could find one, Bruno leaped out of the bushes and tackled him. Then Sid thumped him over the head.

"Good job, boys!" Sid said, picking up the piggy bank. He bashed the bank against a rock and the three dogs gasped as biscuits poured out.

Suddenly Sid's ears perked up. "Shh. What was that?"

They all listened.

"Quick," Sid said. "Someone's coming. Help me get the biscuits into this bag."

The three thieves loaded up the loot and hurried off into the bushes, leaving Ned beside the road.

Coming down the highway was a terrier by the name of Dr. Scotty. He was on his way to perform an operation in Poochville.

As Dr. Scotty rounded the bend, he was surprised to see a dog lying battered and bruised beside the road.

"My, but that dog doesn't appear well," he exclaimed. "I would consider helping him, but I'm already late for my operation. Besides, I wouldn't want to risk getting sick myself."

Hurrying to the opposite side of the road, he continued on his way toward Poochville.

Some time later another traveler came along. It was Prissy Highnose, a poodle from a wealthy family. Prissy's limousine had gotten a flat tire, and she had decided to go on ahead while her chauffeur worked on it.

Rounding the bend in the road, she spotted Ned.

"Oh, my! How dreadful," she exclaimed. "Some poor creature has fallen by the roadside. I suppose I should help him, but I wouldn't want to get mussed up. And besides, what if he is simply pretending to be hurt in order to draw me to his side and then steal my valuables? Well, he won't fool me!"

Lifting her nose high into the air, she continued down the road.

It was late afternoon when an overall-clad traveler pushing an old cart finally happened down the road. It was Nicholas the cat. By now he was over halfway to his family reunion and he was getting more excited with every step.

As his cart slowly rounded the bend in the road, Nicholas saw the large dog lying in the ditch up ahead.

"Uh-oh, thieves hereabout," he said warily. "That unfortunate dog must have fallen prey to them. I wonder . . . should I stop to help him? It could make me late for my reunion. And there is always a chance that this is some sort of trap."

Then Nicholas shook his head. "Those are silly excuses. This poor animal needs my help."

58

Leaning over the injured dog, Nicholas suddenly recognized him. "Why, it's Ned!"he gasped. "And he's been robbed!"

Nicholas carefully bandaged Ned's wounds and put drops of milk on his dry tongue. After straining to load him onto the cart, he summoned all of his strength to push the cart down the road.

Fortunately, it wasn't long before they reached the Dog Tired Inn.

Nicholas entered the Inn and asked about a room. "Do you have any empty rooms?" he asked the clerk.

"Oh, my!" the beagle said. "You're . . . you're a . . ."

"A cat," Nicholas smiled. "Yes, I know. About that room . . ."

"It doesn't make any difference to me, mind you, but . . ." The beagle paused, pointing at a sign near the door.

"No Cats Allowed!" Nicholas read. "But sir, I have a wounded dog outside in my cart."

"Well, then, that changes things, doesn't it? Have you any biscuits?"

Nicholas shook his head. "No, but I do have a load of fresh vegetables."

"Hmmmm. This is highly irregular," the beagle said, rubbing his jowls.

Nicholas finally convinced the innkeeper to give him a room, and then helped Ned into bed. It wasn't until the next morning that Ned awoke.

"Where am I?" Ned grumbled groggily. "And what are you doing here?" he asked when he saw Nicholas standing by his bed with a tray full of food.

"I was on my way to a family reunion when I found you by the road," Nicholas explained. "I'm afraid you were robbed."

"Robbed?" Ned groaned. "And you helped me?"

Nicholas nodded.

"What about all the mean things I've done to you? Barking at you, pestering you?"

"We're still neighbors," Nicholas said, "even if we don't always get along."

"Neighbors, huh?" Ned grunted.

"Neighbors," Nicholas smiled. "Now, eat something before it gets cold. I've got to get back to my farm, but I'll be back to check on you in a few days."

Nicholas paid the innkeeper with vegetables and asked him to take good care of Ned. Then he headed down the road toward Pupland.

A few days later, Nicholas went back to check on Ned. The sheriff was doing much better and felt well enough to return home.

In the coming days the two animals became friends. Nicholas kept farming. And Ned continued to make sure that no one broke the law.

But each Friday, when an overall-clad figure rolled his cart into the town, Ned didn't leap up and block his path. Instead, he rose and cleared the way for the farmer cat.

"Make way, you dogs!" he would yell. And when Nicholas parked his cart in the village square, Ned would announce his arrival. "Gather around, townsdogs! Come and see the fine vegetables of our neighbor, Nicholas the cat!"

You can read a story like this in the Bible. Jesus told it in Luke 10:25-37:

On one occasion an expert in the law stood up to test Jesus. "Teacher," he asked, "what must I do to inherit eternal life?"

"What is written in the Law?" he replied. "How do you read it?"

He answered: " 'Love the Lord your God with all your heart and with all your soul and with all your strength and with all your mind'; and, 'Love your neighbor as yourself.' "

"You have answered correctly," Jesus replied. "Do this and you will live."

But he wanted to justify himself, so he asked Jesus, "And who is my neighbor?"

In reply Jesus said: "A man was going down from Jerusalem to Jericho, when he fell into the hands of robbers. They stripped him of his clothes, beat him, and went away, leaving him half dead. A priest happened to be going down the same road, and when he saw the man, he passed by on the other side. So too, a Levite, when he came to the place and saw him, passed by on the other side. But a Samaritan, as he traveled, came where the man was; and when he saw him, he took pity on him. He went to him and bandaged his wounds, pouring on oil and wine. Then he put the man on his own donkey, took him to an inn, and took care of him. The next day he took out two silver coins and gave them to the innkeeper. 'Look after him,' he said, 'and when I return, I will reimburse you for any extra expense you may have.'

"Which of these three do you think was a neighbor to the man who fell into the hands of robbers?"

The expert in the law replied, "The one who had mercy on him."

Jesus told him, "Go and do likewise."

King Leonard's Celebration

The Great Banquet
Luke 14:15-24

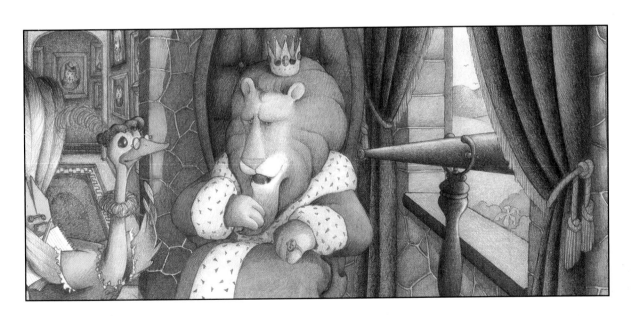

There was once a lion king who ruled over all the beasts of the jungle. His name was Leonard, and he lived in a majestic castle high atop a mountain in the center of a jungle. He seldom came down from his beautiful palace, but kept watch over his subjects by gazing through his royal telescope.

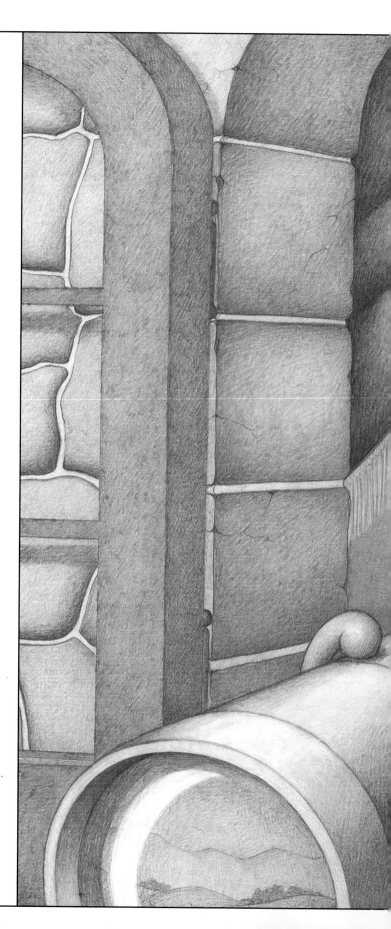

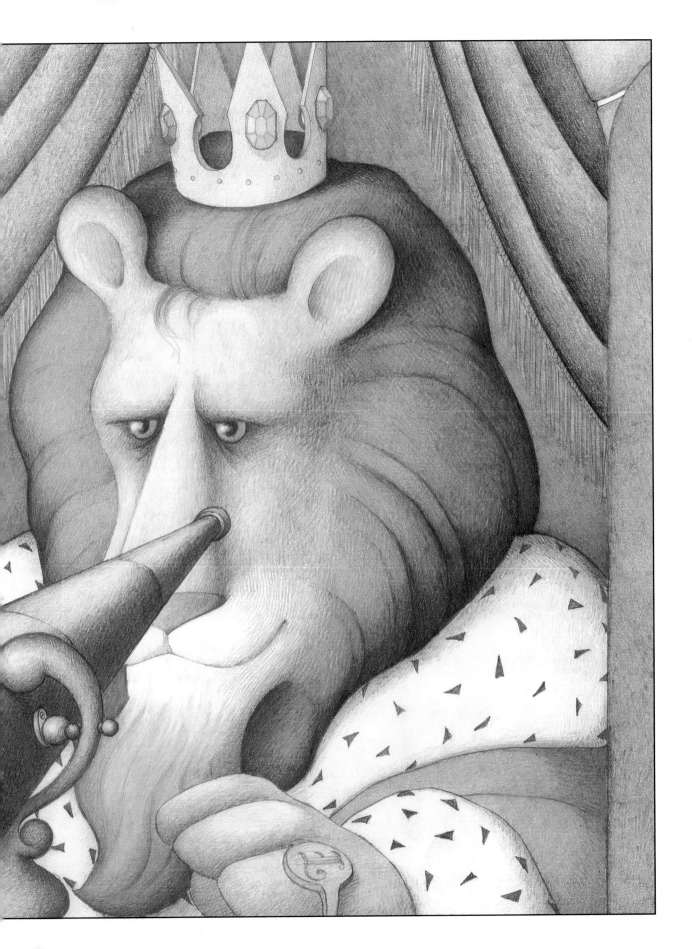

One fine summer day as King Leonard sat upon his throne, he had an idea.

"Horatio!" the king bellowed, nearly losing his crown.

A few moments later a tall, thin bird scurried up to the throne.

"You called, Sire?" the bird asked.

"Yes, Horatio," King Leonard began. "I have had a wonderful idea. I would like to give my subjects an extra-special celebration. There shall be fine foods, games, balloons, cakes, music, noisemakers, puzzles, and . . . ice cream! Yes! Prepare gallons and gallons of ice cream."

"But, Sire," Horatio said, "where will you hold this celebration?"

"I will invite all of the animals here to my palace," the king smiled.

"Here, Sire?" the bird frowned. "But they have never. . . ."

"I know," the king nodded. "They have never been here before. Well, it is high time that they came. We will hold the party tomorrow. Begin the preparations immediately."

So a royal decree was issued and the king's fleet-footed messengers ran to and fro, passing out invitations to all the jungle animals.

One messenger went to Henry Hyena's home.

"What do you want?" Henry asked when he answered the door.

"Mr. Hyena," the messenger explained, "King Leonard has requested your presence at a royal celebration which will...."

"King?" Henry chuckled. "King schming! You don't expect me to believe that nonsense, do you? King Leonard is a joke. He's not real. Nobody's ever even seen him."

Then I take it you won't be attending his party?" the messenger asked.

"You don't give up, do you?" Henry laughed. "I'd really like to," he jested, "but I just bought the Sahara Desert and thought I'd go take a look at it. Get it? I bought the Sahara Desert...."

And before the royal messenger could say another word, Henry slammed the door in his face.

At the house of Zelda the Zebra, another messenger was knocking at the door. His arrival was announced by the barking of Ms. Zebra's two energetic dogs.

"Who is it?" she asked without opening the door.

"A royal messenger come to invite you to King Leonard's celebration," the messenger said. "There will be music and plenty of food and. . . ."

"Are you telling me that that mean old lion is having a party?!" Zelda exclaimed. "I suppose I'm to be the main course."

"Oh, no," the messenger tried to explain. "Certainly not."

"Listen," Zelda said sternly. "I just bought a pair of fierce watchdogs and I'll be too busy teaching them to attack intruders to go to any party."

"Then good day to you, Ma'am," the messenger said, marking Ms. Zebra's name off of his list.

Another messenger approached the house of Marvin Monkey and rang the doorbell.

After a brief pause, the door opened and out swung Marvin.

"Good morning, Mr. Monkey," the messenger said brightly. "I have come to ask if you would like to attend King Leonard's celebration."

"Nah," Marvin shook his head. "Me and the missis just got hitched."

"Well, congratulations," the messenger said.

"So we ain't comin'," the monkey said, and he turned to scamper back up the vine.

"I'm sure the king will be disappointed," the royal messenger called after him.

But Marvin had already swung into the house and slammed the door behind him.

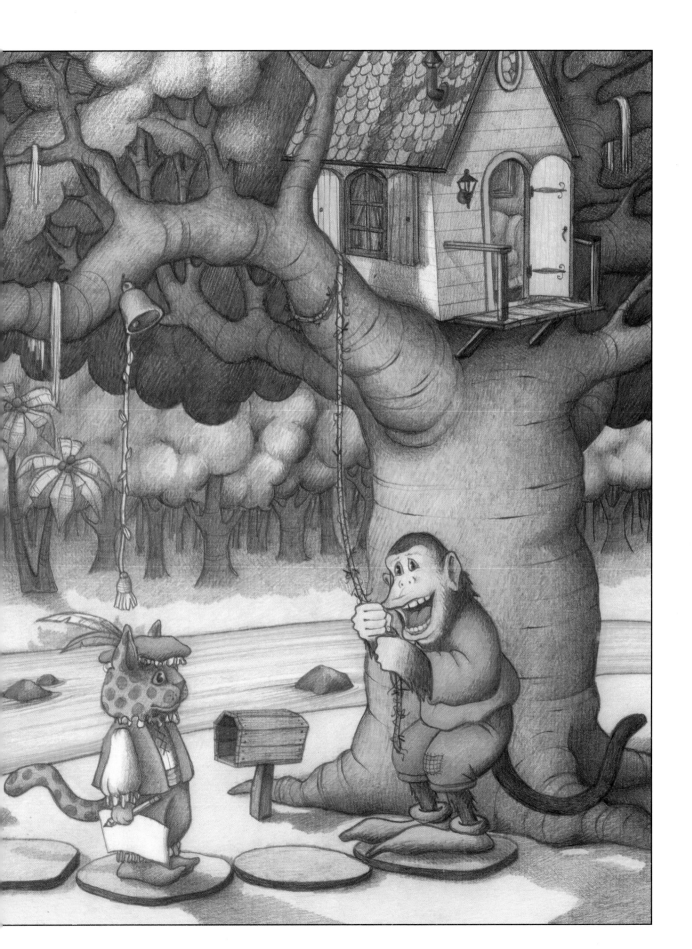

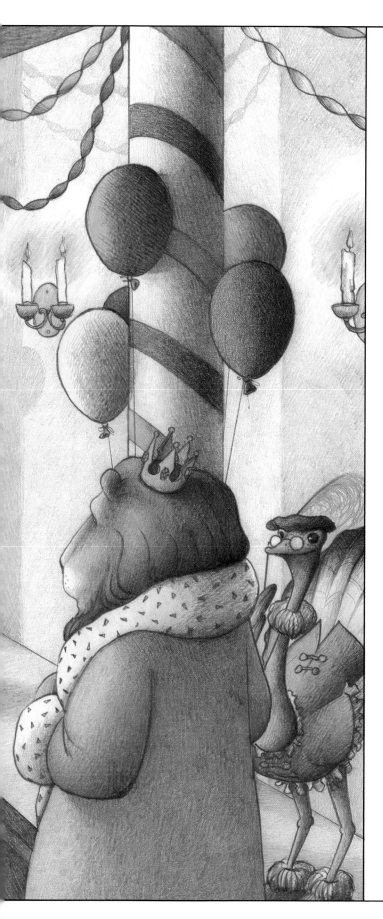

Meanwhile, back at the palace, King Leonard was pleased to see that the preparations in the grand ballroom were nearly complete.

"Good afternoon, Sire," Horatio said with a salute. "The royal dessert-makers are ready to commence with the ice cream at your word."

King Leonard turned to the cluster of cooks waiting near the ice-cream-making equipment.

"Gentlemen," the king said, raising his paw into the air, "let the ice cream begin!"

This sent the cooks into a frenzy of measuring, pouring, and stirring.

"You have done a fine job, Horatio," the king said, patting the thin bird on the back. "A fine job indeed."

Just then one of the royal messengers came in and whispered something to Horatio.

"I'm afraid I have some bad news, Sire," the thin bird said with a frown.

"What is it?" the king asked. "Are any of my subjects unable to attend the celebration?"

Horatio nodded and began reading from a list the messenger had handed him.

Henry Hyena, Zelda the Zebra, Marvin the Monkey . . ." he read.

"How terrible," the King exclaimed.

"Wally Water Buffalo, Sam the Snake and his sister Susie, Hubert Hippopotamus, Elizabeth the Elephant . . ."

"O my," the king moaned, putting a paw over his face.

"Patricia Panther, Charles the Cheetah, Oliver the Orangutan, Gregory Gorilla . . ."

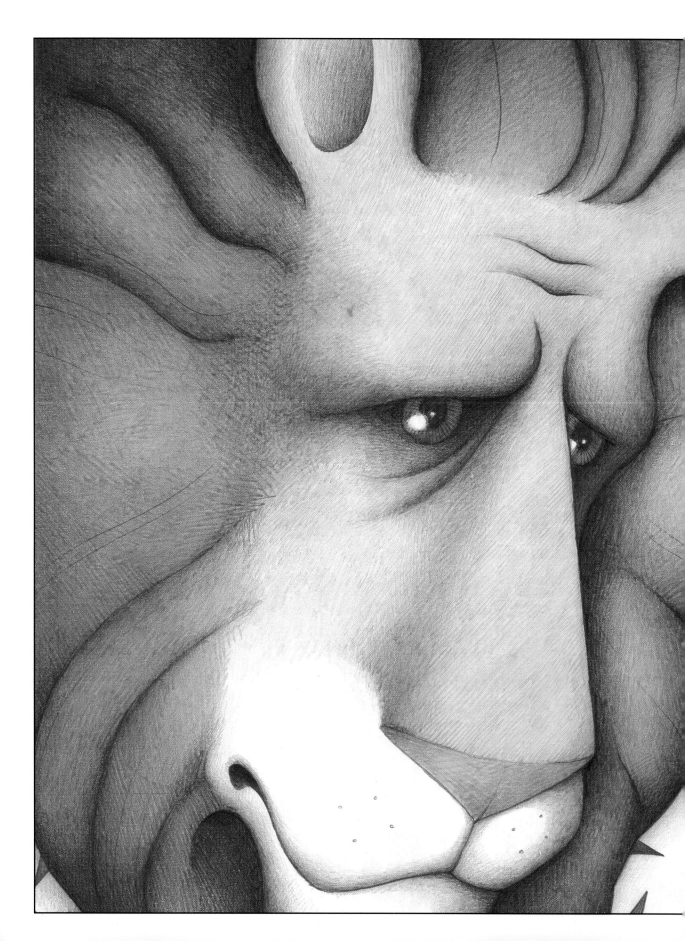

"None of them will be attending?" King Leonard asked, his face filled with disappointment. "Then tell me Horatio, who can come?"

"No one, Sire," the thin bird said quietly. "No one will be coming to your celebration."

Horatio had never seen King Leonard look so sad.

"I am very sorry, Sire," the bird said, trying to comfort the king. "Would you like me to have the decorations taken down and the food put into the royal refrigerators?"

The king nodded glumly.

"And what shall I do about the ice cream, Sire?" he asked.

"It will certainly not save," the king said with a sigh. "It must be disposed of. See to it."

Horatio was about to carry out the order when King Leonard had another idea.

"Wait, Horatio!" the king roared. "Allow the cooks to continue with the royal ice cream."

"But, Sire, who will eat it?" Horatio asked.

King Leonard stroked his mane and thought out loud. "My own subjects will not attend, eh? Then we shall carry on without them. Summon my messengers once again."

Horatio saluted and bowed. "Royal messengers!" he squawked.

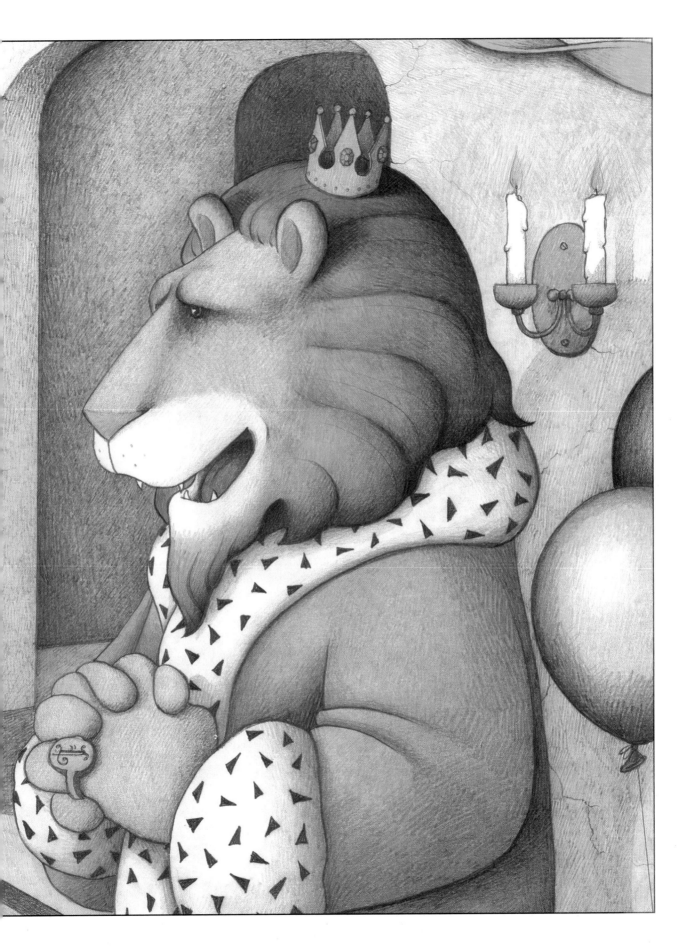

The king's fleet-footed messengers were sent out again to deliver invitations for the royal celebration. But this time, by the king's order, they journeyed beyond the jungle to the great towns of the forest, and even as far as the cities by the sea. As they went, they handed out invitations for King Leonard's party to everyone they met.

Many of these animals were dirty; some had only rags for clothes. Yet they skipped about with joy when they heard the news and gladly agreed to attend the celebration. Then they happily followed the messengers to the king's palace where they were given baths and beautiful clothes to wear.

"Sire," Horatio addressed the king. "The messengers have carried out your request."

King Leonard raised his furry eyebrows. "And have they returned with partygoers?"

Horatio nodded proudly.

The king clapped his paws together.

"But, Sire," the bird said, "there are still a few empty seats at the banquet table. And the ice cream is almost ready."

"Call for the royal messengers again," the king said. "Send them to . . . the country. And tell them to be quick!"

Horatio disappeared in a flurry of feathers and sent the messengers one last time. They went to the country, just as the king had commanded, inviting all the animals they could find.

When every seat at the banquet table had been filled, King Leonard entered the royal ballroom. He was delighted with what he saw. There, in the midst of the festive decorations, was a host of smiling faces eagerly awaiting the start of the celebration.

Upon seeing the king, the guests gasped with surprise and wonder. Then they stood and bowed before him.

"Greetings, my new friends," King Leonard called out in a regal voice.

"Greetings, Your Highness," they responded politely.

Stepping to his seat, King Leonard lifted his punch-filled goblet high into the air. "I welcome you all to my palace. Let the celebration begin!"

To the animals' surprise, balloons suddenly dropped from the high ceiling and bright fireworks exploded. It was all quite delightful, and the crowd joined in, shouting and blowing noisemakers and tooters.

Above the roar of the crowd, King Leonard addressed the royal band. "Let there be music!"

The music and games began, and the ballroom was filled with happy sounds. Then Horatio spoke a word in the king's ear. The lion smiled and jumped up from his seat. "My dear guests," he said with a cublike grin, "the royal ice cream is now ready to be served!"

At this the crowd cheered.

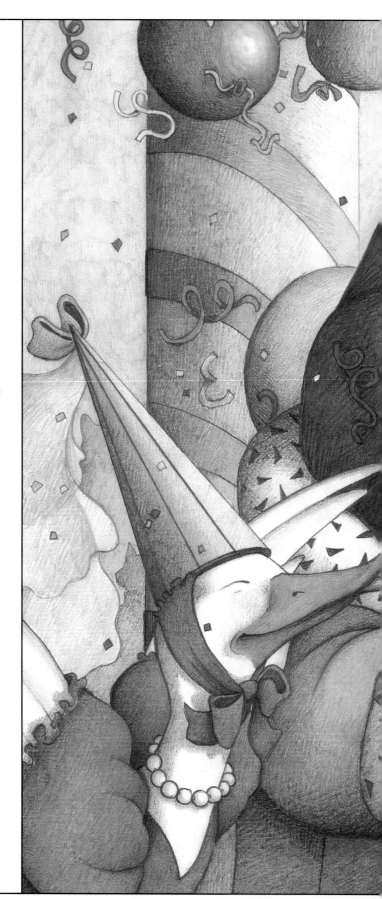

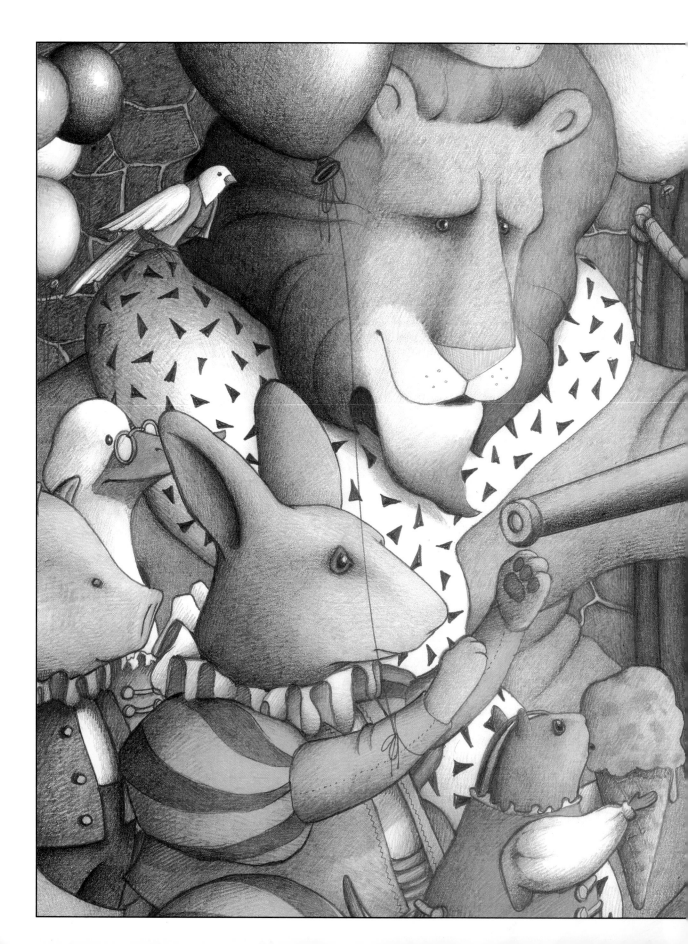

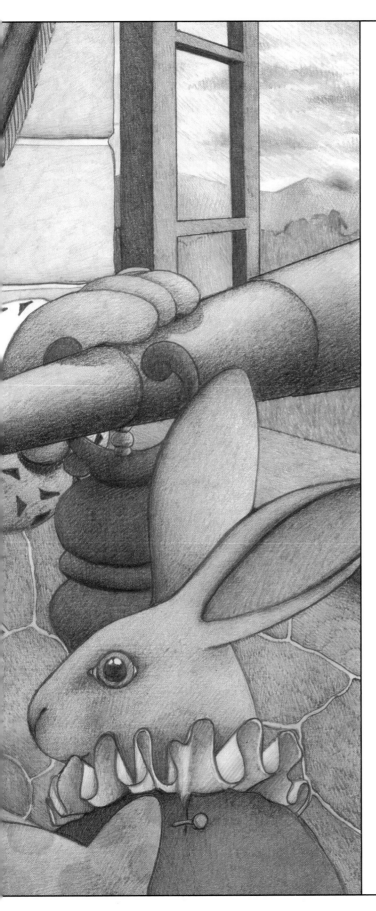

So it was that King Leonard's celebration began. And what a celebration it was. The king talked with his new friends, walked with them, shared in their games, and even let them look through his royal telescope.

The animals had a splendid time as well!. In fact, they so enjoyed the company of the king that they did not want to return to their own homes. In the end, King Leonard invited them all to stay and live with him in his palace.

So the party was extended. Day after day, the king and his new friends played, sang, and ate ice cream. And day after day, King Leonard's celebration continued.

You can read a story like this in the Bible. Jesus told it in Luke 14:15-24:

When one of those at the table with him heard this, he said to Jesus, "Blessed is the man who will eat at the feast in the kingdom of God."

Jesus replied: "A certain man was preparing a great banquet and invited many guests. At the time of the banquet he sent his servant to tell those who had been invited, 'Come, for everything is now ready.'

"But they all alike began to make excuses. The first said, 'I have just bought a field, and I must go and see it. Please excuse me.'

"Another said, 'I have just bought five yoke of oxen, and I'm on my way to try them out. Please excuse me.'

"Still another said, 'I just got married, so I can't come.'

"The servant came back and reported this to his master. Then the owner of the house became angry and ordered his servant, 'Go out quickly into the streets and alleys of the town and bring in the poor, the crippled, the blind, and the lame.'

" 'Sir,' the servant said, 'what you ordered has been done, but there is still room.'

"Then the master told his servant, 'Go out to the roads and country lanes and make them come in, so that my house will be full. I tell you, not one of those men who were invited will get a taste of my banquet.' "

Cornelius T. Mouse and Sons

The Prodigal Son
Luke 15:11-32

There was once a mouse named Cornelius who lived with his two sons, Samuel and Timothy, on an estate in the countryside. Cornelius was a very prosperous mouse who owned a thriving apple orchard and operated a cheeseworks where cheese was made.

He and his sons lived in a large home atop a grass-covered hill overlooking the estate. Their house had many rooms, but Cornelius' favorite was the library. Many an evening would find Cornelius seated in the library, reading away the hours.

While Cornelius was quite proud of his estate, his orchard, and his cheeseworks, he was most proud of his sons Samuel and Timothy. Cornelius loved and prized them above all else.

Samuel, his oldest son, was a serious sort who had taken a keen interest in cheesemaking. His younger brother Timothy, on the other hand, had absolutely no interest in work of any kind. Yet despite this lack of interest, Timothy had an eye for apples and worked in the orchard.

One fall afternoon, Cornelius finished his work early and set off for the library.

With a mug of cider by his side, he browsed the shelves for something to read. He finally selected a fine little book and had just settled into his chair when there came a tap at the door.

"Come in," he said.

"Sir," his housekeeper, Mrs. Wiggins, said as she opened the door, "the Beaver brothers are here with your sign."

"Oh, very good," Cornelius said excitedly. "Let's have a look."

The beavers carried in an oak sign which had been skillfully engraved with tall, stylish letters. It read: "Cornelius T. Mouse & Sons: Apples by the Bushel and Cheese by the Wheel."

"My, but it's handsome," Cornelius said. "Won't the boys be surprised?"

That evening after supper, Cornelius brought a cloth-covered stand into the dining room.

"Sons, I am pleased to announce the formation of a new company," he said, pulling the cloth from the sign.

"Cornelius T. Mouse & Sons," the two young mice read in unison, "Apples by the Bushel and Cheese by the Wheel."

"Samuel, henceforth you shall be my head cheesemaker," he stated proudly, "and, Timothy, you shall be my chief appler."

Then he pulled two gold rings from his pocket and placed them on his sons' fingers. "To signify our new partnership," he explained.

"Thank you, Father," Samuel said with wide eyes.

But Timothy didn't say anything. He just stared out the window.

"Is something bothering you, Timothy?" Cornelius asked.

"I don't want to be your partner," Timothy said. "Now that I'm grown, I want to move to the city."

Cornelius blinked several times, and his legs began to wobble.

"Perhaps you could give me my share of the business in coins, Father. That would put me well on my way."

Cornelius silently led Timothy upstairs to his study. Opening his money box he counted out a tall stack of gold coins.

"Be careful with these," he warned. "They are your inheritance. Not something to be spent foolishly."

The young mouse nodded and accepted the money.

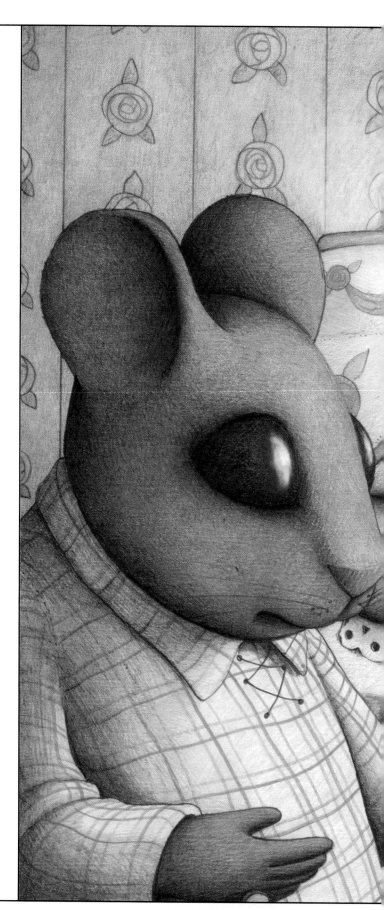

Early the next morning, Timothy left for the city of Varmintsville.

It was a long trip, but when the stagecoach finally rolled into town, he took one look around and decided that it would be a wonderful place to live.

Timothy wasted no time establishing himself in his new home. He took a room in the best hotel in town and immediately went on a shopping expedition. He bought all sorts of fine clothes, jewelry, and nifty gadgets. Everywhere he went, he bought whatever pleased his eye.

And that evening, Timothy threw a wonderful party, ordering cartloads of snacks, exotic fruits and drinks, cakes and pastries. He even hired a band of rats to provide music.

Back at the estate, Cornelius was very worried about Timothy. And as the days passed, he found it difficult to keep his mind on his work. During the daylight hours, he would often walk to the main road and look to see if his son was returning. Many an evening he would skip his supper and head straight to bed. But try as he might, he could not get to sleep.

Meanwhile, Timothy continued shopping and throwing wild parties until one morning he found that he had spent his entire fortune in a few short weeks.

In order to pay his bills, he had to return the things he had bought and was even forced to give up his gold ring, the one his father had given him.

He was tossed out of his hotel and wandered aimlessly from street to street until he happened upon one of his city friends.

"Timothy!" his friend said. "Boy, am I ever glad to see you. I've really been down on my luck. Could you spare some change?"

Of course Timothy couldn't help him. And when his other friends heard that he would no longer be throwing nightly parties, they deserted him. He was left poor and all alone on the streets of Varmintsville.

That very day Cornelius had been sitting at his desk trying to do his work. Yet he could not keep his mind on business.

"You're worried about that young mouse of yours, aren't you?" Mrs. Wiggins asked as she brought him a tray of snacks.

Cornelius nodded.

"If I might offer a suggestion, sir," she said, "perhaps you could take your carriage out for a ride."

"I have work to do," Cornelius said flatly. "And I am in no mood for a ride."

"Even if the drive were in the direction of say . . . Varmintsville?"

"A sterling idea, Mrs. Wiggins!" Cornelius cried.

Minutes later Cornelius had hooked up his horse and was flying down the road.

Back in Varmintsville, Timothy was getting hungrier and hungrier. Just when he was about to give up hope, he noticed a sign which read "Help Wanted." He asked about it and was given a job serving tables in an eatery.

The restaurant was called "The Slop Shoppe," and Timothy soon discovered why. The customers were pigs. His job was to carry large platters piled high with slop out to the porky patrons.

As Timothy served the hungry hogs day after day, he came to a decision.

"I would quite prefer my old life in the country to this," he said. "I wonder if my father would take me back as an apprentice appletender? I do believe it's worth finding out."

So when the pigs were busy gulping down slop, Timothy made his apologies to the owner and left.

Cornelius was nearing Varmintsville when he decided to stop for lunch. Spreading out a blanket, he sat down on the crest of a hill to nibble on some cheese.

While he was munching, he spotted something down the road. He soon realized that the something was a someone, a small animal walking toward him.

"Could it be?" Cornelius wondered. "It is!" he shouted, running down the hill. "Timothy, my son!"

Timothy's stomach was growling and his feet were weary from walking. But as he looked up and saw an animal running toward him, flailing its arms, he forgot about how tired and hungry he was.

Could it be? he wondered.

"It is!" he shouted. "Father!" And he scurried up the hill to meet him.

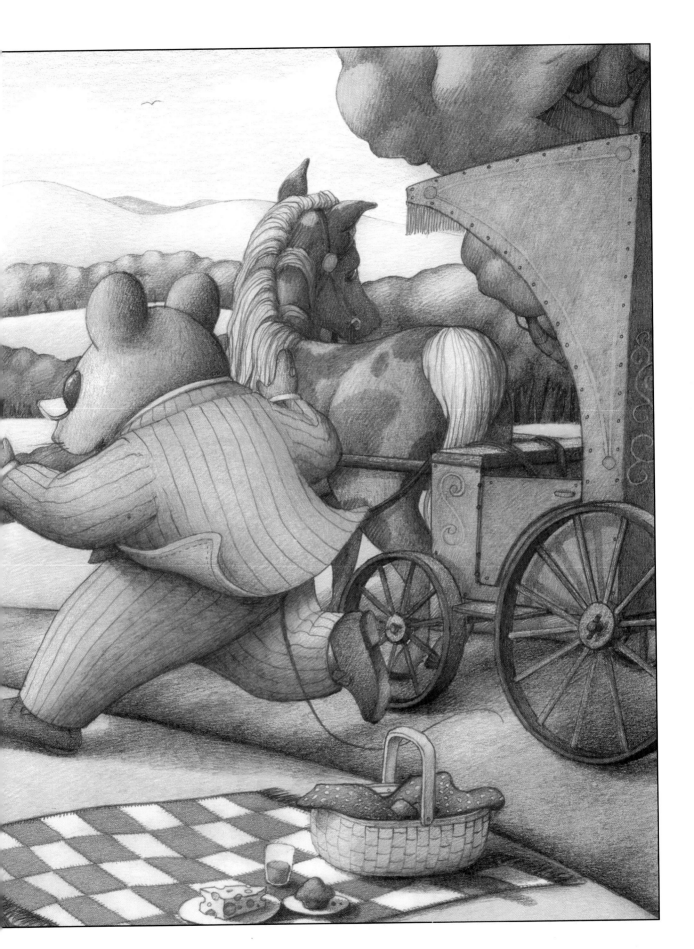

Moments later the two mice were hugging and exchanging kisses.

"Father, I'm so sorry," Timothy blubbered. "I lost my inheritance. I even lost your ring." He hung his head. "I'm not worthy to be your son. But might I return as an apprentice appletender?"

Cornelius lifted Timothy's head with his paw. "You will always be my son. And any son of mine deserves nothing less than a full partnership!"

Timothy's eyes widened in amazement.

"About that ring," Cornelius said, pulling the gold band from his own finger, "here — take mine."

Cornelius and Timothy raced home in the carriage. When they arrived at the estate, Cornelius ordered Mrs. Wiggins to prepare an extra-special-occasion supper and invite all of the neighbors to celebrate Timothy's homecoming.

Samuel, who had been hard at work in the cheeseworks, returned just as the party began. Hearing music, he looked in through the window and saw a crowd of animals laughing and eating.

"What's all the fuss?" he asked Mrs. Wiggins.

"Oh, Samuel, it's so exciting," the kindly kangaroo rat said. "Your brother Timothy has come home!"

"Is that all?" he grumbled. "A fool's return is no reason to celebrate."

"But won't you come in to the party?" Mrs. Wiggins asked.

"I believe I'll stay out here, thank you," Samuel answered snootily.

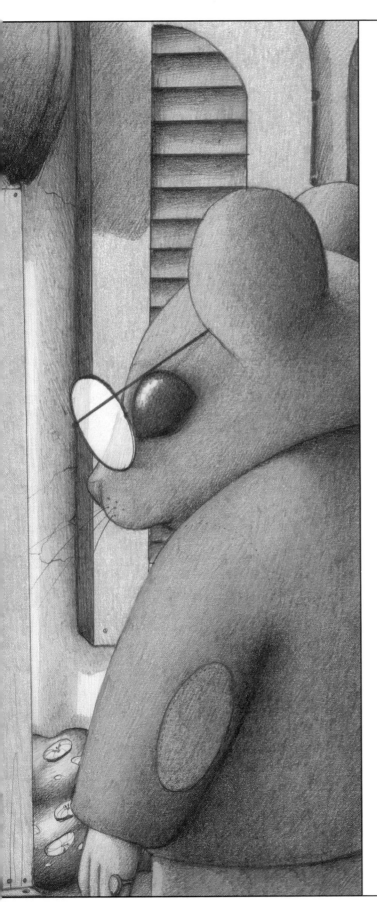

Cornelius soon came out to talk with Samuel.

"Why won't you rejoice with us?" Cornelius asked him.

"All these years I've worked for you, Father," Samuel complained, "and you've never thrown me a party. Yet Timothy leaves home and wastes his inheritance and. . . ."

"Samuel, my dear son," Cornelius said with a smile, "all that I have is yours. But your brother was as good as gone, and now he has come back to us. We must celebrate."

Samuel frowned. He understood, but he didn't think it was fair. Though he wasn't happy about it, he followed his father inside and shook hands with Timothy.

The next day, after the party was over, Cornelius called Samuel and Timothy into his study.

"Now," he said with a smile, "let the three of us work together to make Cornelius T. Mouse & Sons a success."

And in the following days, they did just that.

You can read a story like this in the Bible. Jesus told it in Luke 15:11-32:

There was a man who had two sons. The younger one said to his father, "Father, give me my share of the estate." So he divided his property between them.

Not long after that, the younger son got together all he had, set off for a distant country, and there squandered his wealth in wild living. After he had spent everything, there was a severe famine in that whole country, and he began to be in need. So he went and hired himself out to a citizen of that country, who sent him to his fields to feed pigs. He longed to fill his stomach with the pods that the pigs were eating, but no one gave him anything.

When he came to his senses, he said, "How many of my father's hired men have food to spare, and here I am starving to death! I will set out and go back to my father and say to him: 'Father, I have sinned against heaven and against you. I am no longer worthy to be called your son; make me like one of your hired men.' " So he got up and went to his father.

But while he was still a long way off, his father saw him and was filled with compassion for him; he ran to his son, threw his arms around him, and kissed him.

The son said to him, "Father, I have sinned against heaven and against you. I am no longer worthy to be called your son."

But the father said to his servants. "Quick! Bring the best robe and put it on him. Put a ring on his finger and sandals on his feet. Bring the fattened calf and kill it. Let's have a feast and celebrate. For this son of mine was dead and is alive again; he was lost and is found." So they began to celebrate. . . .

Mrs. Beaver and the Wolf at the Door

The Persistent Widow
Luke 18:1-7

There was once a beaver named Barney who lived with his wife Beatrice on a pond at the edge of the forest. Their beautiful home was made out of fine logs which Barney had selected himself, diligently chewed to fit, and carefully set into place. Beatrice had taken charge of the inside of the house, pasting up wallpaper in the kitchen, painting the rooms pleasant shades, and hanging curtains. Together, Mr. and Mrs. Beaver had built a warm, cozy home in which to live.

It came about one day that tragedy struck. Barney fell off the roof. A doctor was summoned, but the poor beaver didn't live through the night.

The next day animals from across the land gathered at the Beaver home. Sir Humphrey, the wealthy businessbear, addressed the crowd with a few words about Mr. Beaver.

"Those who knew Barney," the bear growled, "loved Barney. A kinder, more faithful animal you couldn't hope to meet. We will all miss him dearly."

When her friends and family had returned to their own homes, Beatrice sat inside her house and cried for a whole week straight. She was so sad and lonely that she cried until she felt she could cry no longer, and then she cried some more.

One day, after her sniffles had finally passed, there came a knock at the door. After checking her face and fur in the hall mirror, Beatrice opened the door to find two animals outside.

"After we get rid of this old house," a weasel was saying to a large wolf in a top hat, "your hotel will fit neatly here next to the pond. I can see it now—'The Wolf's Den Hotel.'"

"Ahem." Beatrice cleared her throat to gain their attention. "Is there something I can help you with?"

"Good day, Madame," the weasel said with a smile. "This will explain everything." And he handed her a sheet of paper.

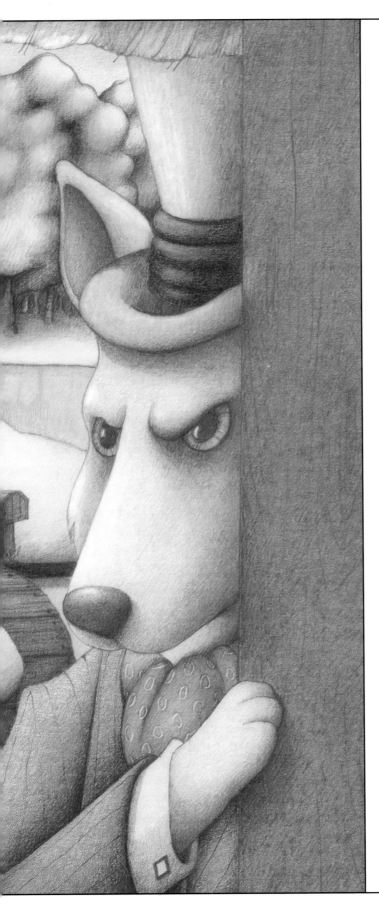

The note said: "Your home is now the property of the J.B. Wolf Company. You and all of your possessions must be off the premises by tomorrow, or else!"

"What!" Beatrice was shocked. "You can't do this. This is my home!"

"Was your home," the weasel said, shuffling through a file of papers. "Says right here that after your husband died, the title deed was transferred to our company."

"I insist on speaking with your superior!" Beatrice demanded.

"Let me introduce myself," the wolf smiled, stepping forward. "Mr. J.B. Wolf, robber baron extraordinaire. My good, Mrs. Beaver, I am afraid that your house is now my property."

"We'll see about that," Beatrice said, trying to sound brave. But after closing the door, she felt like crying.

"Sir Humphrey," she suddenly thought. "If anyone can help me, he can."

Beatrice scurried off through the forest to Sir Humphrey's mansion. But when she arrived she was disappointed to find that he was not at home.

She was about to give up hope when Reginald, Sir Humphrey's butler, suggested that she see Judge Kensington. The butler explained that the judge was a wise elk who settled various arguments between woodland creatures.

Beatrice thanked Reginald and set out to find the judge.

When she arrived at the courthouse, Beatrice introduced herself to the receptionist.

"My name is Mrs. Beatrice Beaver and I must see Judge Kensington," she told the young crow.

"Do you have an appointment?" the bird cawed sleepily.

"No, but it is a matter of some urgency," Beatrice explained.

The crow leafed lazily through a calendar on her desk. "How's two weeks from next Thursday sound?"

"That's much too late," Beatrice objected.

The crow ignored this and began primping her feathers.

Beatrice didn't know what to do. But she knew that she needed to see the judge.

When the crow wasn't looking, Beatrice slipped out of the courthouse and went around to the back. There she found a service entrance used by the maids and cooks. She tiptoed through it and found herself in a long hallway with many doors. Walking quietly down the hall, she eventually came to a door which had a plaque on it. The plaque read: "Behind this door sits a fair judge committed to what is right and just."

Beatrice tapped on the door lightly. When no one answered, she gave it a sharp rap.

Then she spotted a window above the door.

"If only I had a ladder," she thought. But there was nothing in the hall except a serving cart filled with dirty dishes.

Removing the dishes from the cart, she wheeled it in front of the door. Climbing up onto it, she steadied herself with her tail and strained to look through the high window. What she saw was a gray-haired elk wearing a pair of round spectacles. Squinting to get a better look, she noticed that his eyes were closed. The judge was dozing!

Suddenly the cart began to roll and Beatrice lost her balance. Gripping the edge of the window sill, she hung on with all her might.

"Help!" she screamed.

This startled the judge, who jumped out of his chair and came running out of his office at a gallop—only to have Beatrice fall into his arms as he passed through the doorway.

"What? Who are you?" the surprised elk asked as he put her down.

By this time the crow from the entryway had arrived on the scene along with a collection of servants and cooks.

"My name is Mrs. Beatrice Beaver and I have an urgent request, your Honor," she blurted out.

"Make an appointment like everyone else," the judge grumbled. "Now where was I?" he asked himself as he returned to his office and slammed the door.

Sitting on the steps of the courthouse, Beatrice wondered what to do. She was about to head for home when she heard a door close behind her. Turning around, she saw the judge leaving the courthouse.

Beatrice followed him down the path. "Judge Kensington, I must see you!" she pled.

"Oh, not you again," the elk shook his head.

"It's urgent! I must talk with you today!"

"I'm going home," he snorted. "I suggest you do the same." And he walked away at a brisk pace.

Beatrice had to run just to keep the elk in sight.

When the judge reached his home, he hurried inside, leaving Beatrice standing in the street. He gave a sigh of relief, thinking he was rid of the pesky beaver. But he was mistaken.

First there was a knock at the door. The judge didn't answer it. Then there came a tapping at the window. So the judge drew the curtains. Next a rock with a note attached to it came bouncing down the chimney. But he refused to read it. Then he heard a noise outside.

"Judge Kensington!" Beatrice hollered at the top of her voice. "Please hear my request!"

Beatrice was making such a racket that the judge threw open the door.

"Stop it!" the judge begged. "I'll do anything you ask, Mrs. Beaver! I'll see to it that your request is granted, if only you will promise to leave me alone."

Beatrice nodded her head in agreement and then explained her problem to the grumpy elk. When she finished, she showed him the note she had been given by the weasel and the wolf.

"Here," the elk said, scribbling a message on the bottom of the notice. "This will take care of the problem. Now I insist that you leave me alone!" And he trotted back inside and slammed the door.

By the time Beatrice reached her home it was very late and she was quite tired. So she went directly to bed.

But early the next morning she heard a knock at the door. Hopping up, she checked her face and fur in the hall mirror and answered the door.

It was the weasel and the wolf.

"You've got an hour to gather your things and get out!" the weasel said, pointing to a crew of animals waiting outside to demolish her home. "As soon as Mr. Wolf gives them the signal. . . ."

"Well perhaps Mr. Wolf should read this," Beatrice smiled, handing him the notice.

The weasel's jaw dropped as he read it: "This notice is deemed illegal. The J.B. Wolf Company has no right to claim the home of Mrs. Beaver. By order of Judge Kensington, you are hereby required to leave her alone."

With his tail drooping between his legs, the weasel turned and gave the notice to his boss.

The wolf read it quickly and then bared his fangs.

"I should have known not to trust a weasel with a wolf's job," the wolf growled. "You have upset me for the last time."

Just as the wolf lunged, the weasel bolted for the road. The wolf took up chase, snapping at his heels.

"Won't you stay for breakfast," Beatrice called after them, as a peaceful smile spread across her face. But they were already too far away to hear.

You can read a story like this in the Bible.
Jesus told it in Luke 18:1-7:

Then Jesus told His disciples a parable to
show them that they should always pray and
not give up. He said: "In a certain town there
was a judge who neither feared God nor
cared about men. And there was a widow in
that town who kept coming to him with the
plea, 'Grant me justice against my adversary.'

"For some time he refused. But finally he
said to himself, 'Even though I don't fear God
or care about men, yet because this widow
keeps bothering me, I will see that she gets
justice, so that she won't eventually wear me
out with her coming!' "

And the Lord said, "Listen to what the un-
just judge says. And will not God bring about
justice for His chosen ones, who cry out to
Him day and night? Will He keep putting
them off? I tell you, He will see that they get
justice, and quickly."

King Leonard's Great Grape Harvest

The Workers in the Vineyard
Matthew 20:1-16

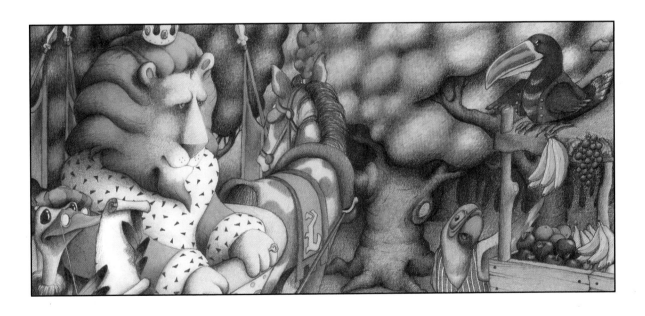

There was once a lion king who ruled over all the beasts of the jungle. His name was Leonard, and he lived in a majestic castle high atop a mountain in the center of a jungle.

Leonard was a very good king and greatly enjoyed doing things for his subjects. It pleased him to give the animals food to eat and clothes to wear. The king loved to watch through his royal telescope as his servants went down into the jungle to deliver barrels of fruit and brightly-wrapped presents.

One sunny afternoon, as King Leonard sat on his throne looking out across the jungle through his royal telescope, he spied his vineyard. He could see that the twisting grapevines had grown long and tall and were now covered with plump, juicy, purple grapes.

"Horatio!" the king roared.

A tall, thin bird scurried up to the throne.

"How may I be of service, Sire?" the bird asked with a salute.

"I have just noticed that my royal vineyard is full of ripe grapes," King Leonard said, turning his gaze toward the polite servant. Then his furry face grew solemn and his regal nose twitched. "These grapes must be picked very soon, or they shall dry up on the vine."

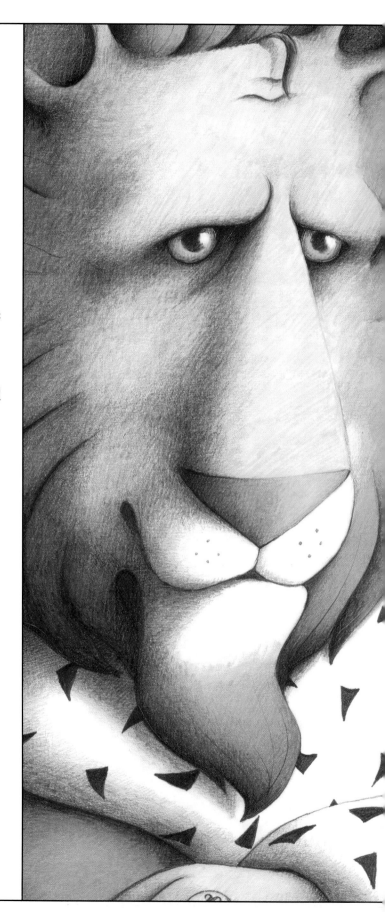

"I will have your servants attend to it immediately, Sire." The bird bowed. "Your vineyard shall be harvested in a week's time."

"The grapes must be picked tomorrow," the king ordered, "or they will spoil."

"But Sire," the thin bird objected, "it would take an army of animals to accomplish such a task."

"Then we must see to it that an army is gathered, Horatio," the king demanded. "Prepare my chariot!"

"But Sire!" Horatio shouted with wide eyes. "You don't intend to—"

"I certainly do," the king said. "Tomorrow we are going down into the jungle to hire animals to pick the grapes in my vineyard."

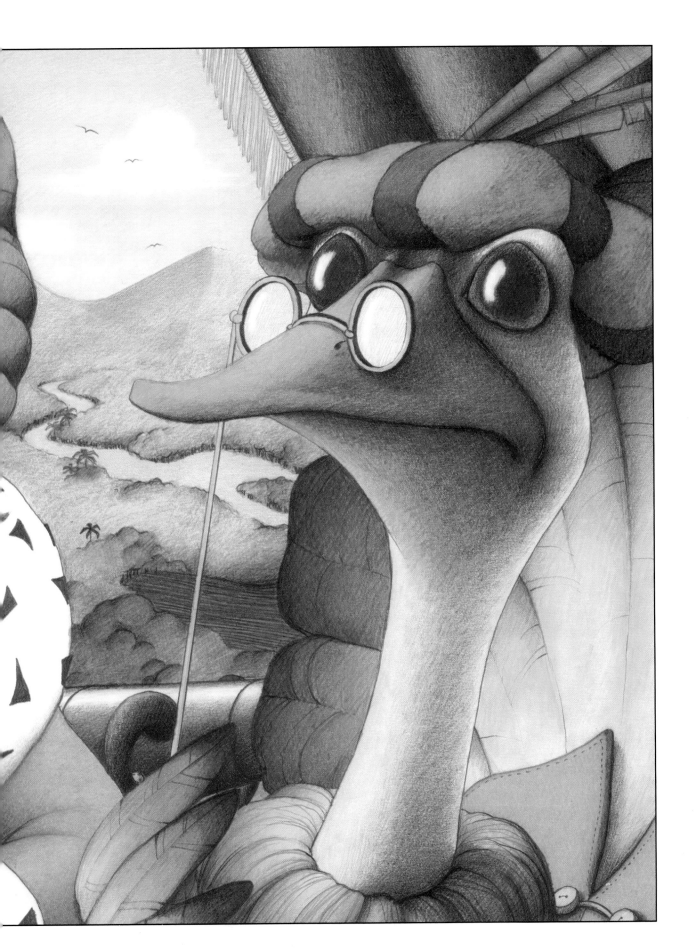

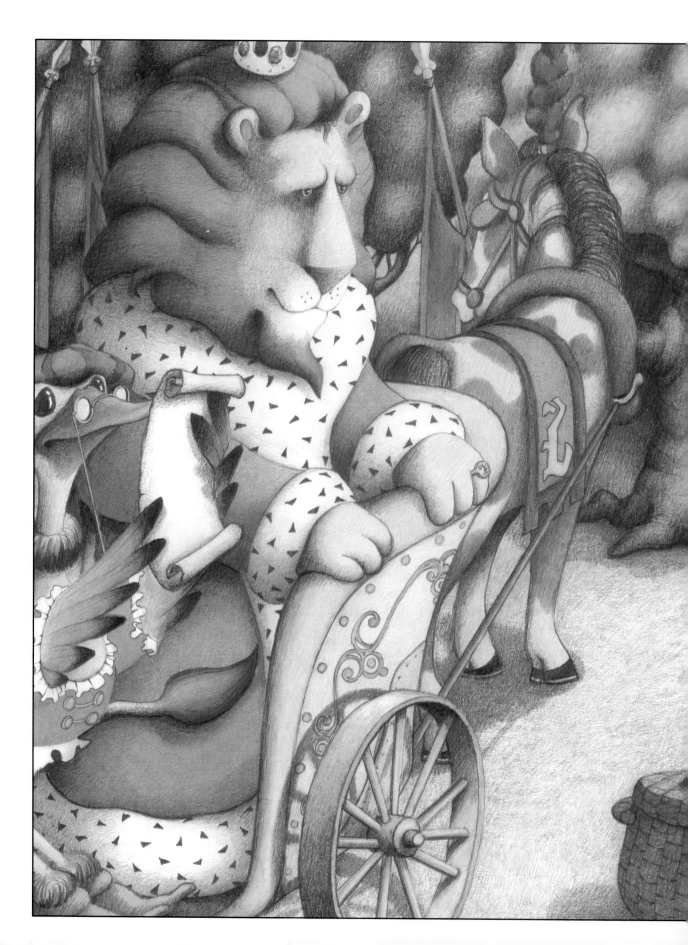

So the royal chariot was prepared, and early the next morning King Leonard rode down from his castle with Horatio at his side. When they reached the marketplace, it was already filled with activity. Birds and snakes and orangutans were setting up stands to sell their wares. And there were a number of other animals just wandering around.

The king's procession came to a halt and the marketplace grew still and quiet. All eyes were drawn to King Leonard.

Horatio rose and lifted his head to announce the king's arrival. "Hear ye, hear ye, all animals of the jungle," he shouted. "The good King Leonard has come down from his castle."

Rising from his chariot, King Leonard prepared to speak. "I have come among you today," the king said in a deep, noble voice, "to offer work to those who are willing."

The animals remained silent, their eyes glued to the regal lion.

"To each of those who will go out into my vineyard and pick grapes today," he said, "I will give one silver coin." He held up a shiny coin for the animals to see.

No one spoke.

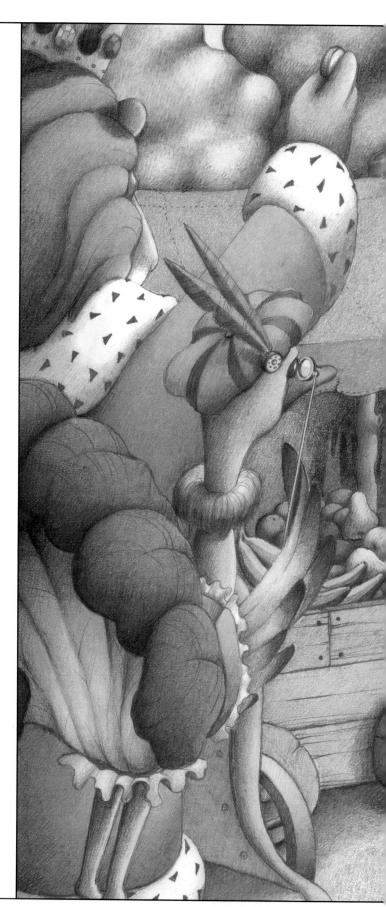

"You there," the king pointed. "My good rhinoceros. Will you work in my vineyard for a silver coin?"

"Why not?" the rhinoceros snorted. "I was just going to hang around all day anyway."

"Very good," the king smiled. "Are there others?"

A gorilla grunted his consent, a leopard leapt forward, a wild boar squealed his approval, and a line began to form next to the king's chariot.

"I wonder if they shall be enough to do the job," the king thought aloud after the animals had been led off toward the vineyard.

"Your vineyard is quite large," Horatio noted. "Perhaps you should hire other workers later in the day to be sure the job will be done by evening."

"A fine idea," the king said. "I shall return every so often and deliver my offer to those who may have missed it. Horatio, have the driver take us once around the jungle."

And the procession began to march forward.

It took King Leonard's chariot the better part of three hours to travel all the way around the jungle, and when they arrived back at the marketplace the king was pleased to find a whole new group of animals.

"Come, work in my vineyard for a silver coin," he told them.

The animals raised their eyebrows as they looked at the shiny coin in the lion's paw and then fell in line behind his chariot.

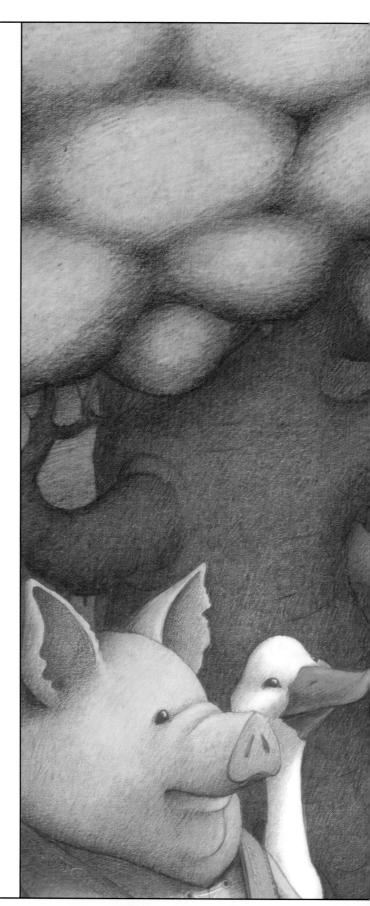

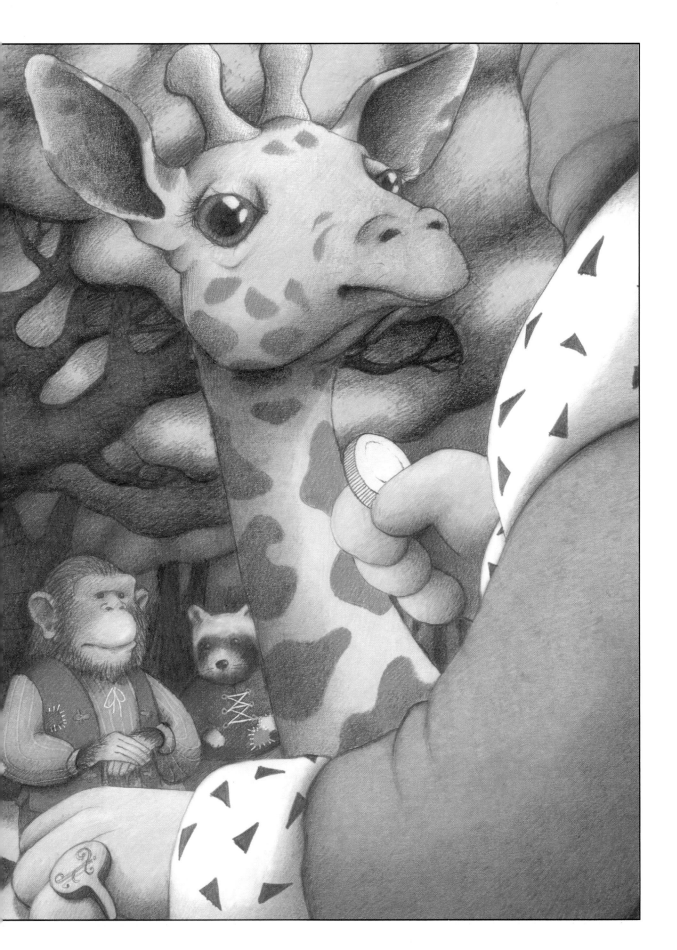

After the new group of workers had been led away to the vineyard, a messenger arrived and whispered something to Horatio.

"I have received news from the vineyard, Sire," the thin bird said to the king.

"Very well," the king nodded, "speak it."

"The workers are picking your grapes," the bird began, "but they will not be able to finish today."

King Leonard let out a long sigh. "Those grapes will spoil by tomorrow. We must have more workers. Take us around the jungle once again."

So the royal procession traveled around the jungle again. And when they arrived back at the marketplace they found still more animals willing to work in the vineyard. This continued all day long. Finally, when it was almost quitting time, the king hired one last group and told them to hurry into the vineyard and pick as many grapes as they could before dark.

Then the waiting began. King Leonard, Horatio, and the royal procession waited in the marketplace for news from the vineyard.

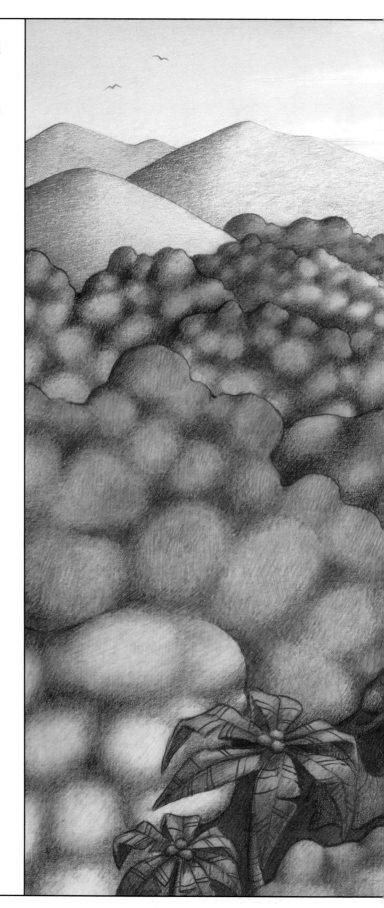

Finally a royal messenger rushed up to Horatio and spoke a word into his ear.

"Sire!" Horatio shouted. "The grapes! They've been picked! Every last one!"

"Hooray!" the king roared.

In a moment the workers began filing into the marketplace. When they all had gathered around the king's chariot, he addressed them.

"My good animals," he began, "you are to be commended for your faithful, diligent work."

He then ordered Horatio to pay them, starting with those who were hired last and ending with those who were hired first.

Things progressed smoothly. The animals hired near quitting time and in the late afternoon were quite happy to receive a silver coin for their few hours of grape-picking.

But when those hired early in the morning reached the front of the line, they began to frown. Having worked much longer than the others, they expected to be paid more. And when the animals King Leonard hired first came to claim their money, they actually scowled and muttered their disapproval.

"Those lazy animals who only worked a few hours got paid as much as we did," the rhinoceros snorted.

"We should have gotten more than just one coin," the wild boar complained.

"It's not fair!" the gorilla grunted, beating his chest.

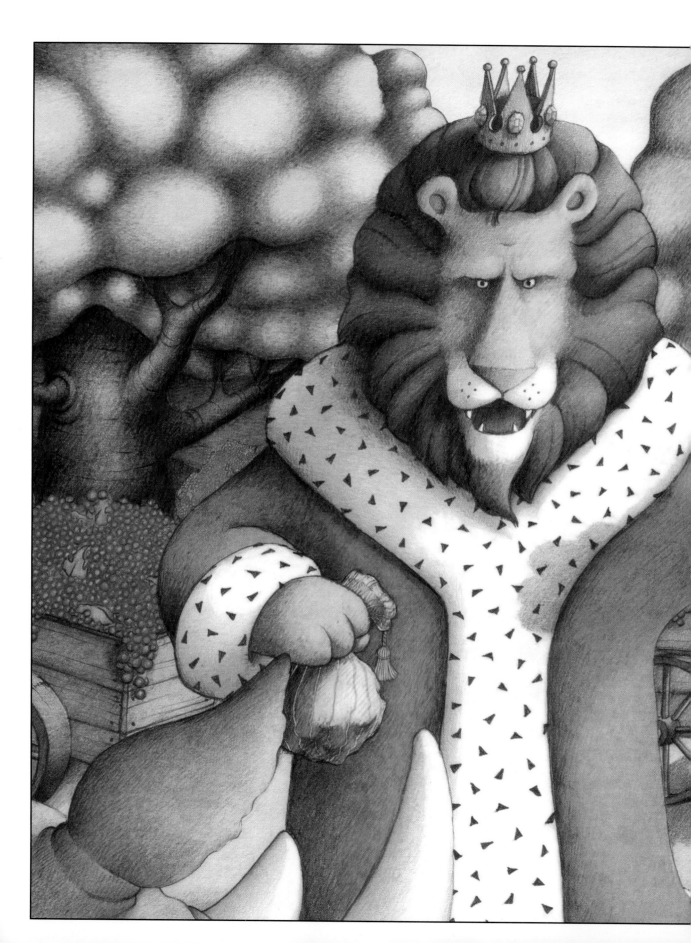

Not fair, indeed!" King Leonard roared. "Did you agree to work in my vineyard for one silver coin?"

"Yes," they nodded.

"Then take your coins and go home," the king said. "I have not cheated you. I am the king," he growled. "And these are my coins. I may do with them as I wish."

The animals turned away with pouty expressions on their faces and slowly made for home.

When the square was finally empty, King Leonard and Horatio sat in the royal chariot, munching on a clump of freshly picked grapes.

"What ever will you do with all of these grapes, Sire?" the thin bird asked between bites.

"Why, give them to my subjects, of course," the lion replied.

"But how could they possibly be delivered?" Horatio wondered. "There are so many."

"Perhaps," the lion said as he gazed at the carts loaded with plump, purple fruit, "perhaps instead of taking the grapes to my subjects, we should bring my subjects to the grapes."

"Sire?" Horatio was puzzled.

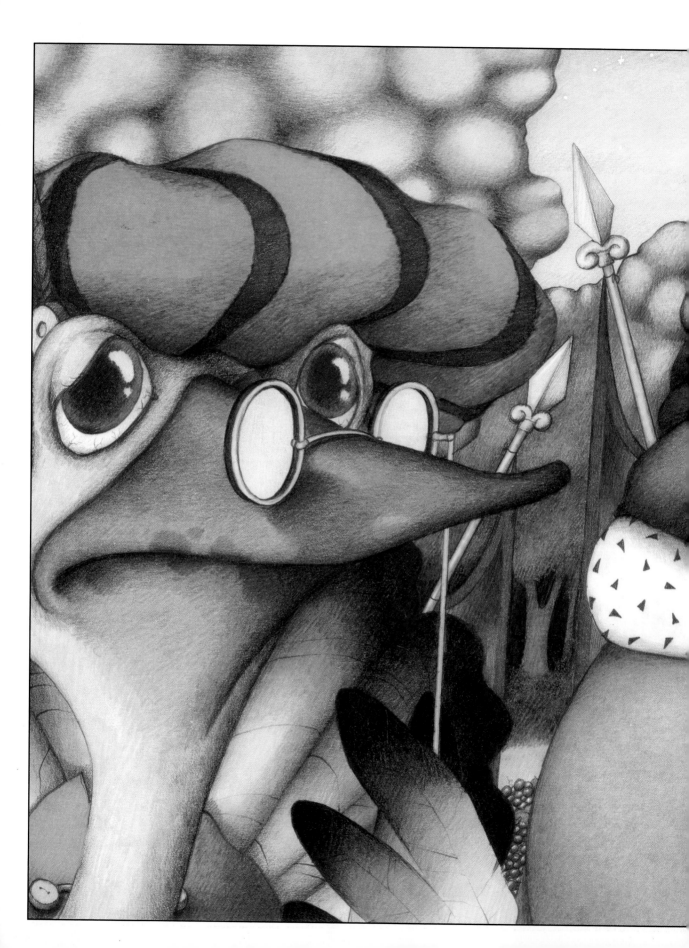

"We shall have a party," the king said excitedly. "Yes, a great grape party for the whole jungle."

"But, Sire—" the bird objected.

"We can have grapes, grape juice, grape jelly..." the king continued. "And grape ice cream!"

Horatio covered his eyes with one wing. "Here we go again," he sighed.

"To the castle," the king roared. "And be quick. There are preparations to make, decorations to be hung, and invitations to be sent out. Isn't it exciting, Horatio?"

"Yes, Sire," the bird groaned, "exciting."

And the royal procession began to march double-time back up to King Leonard's castle to make ready a great grape party for the whole jungle.

You can read a story like this in the Bible. Jesus told it in Matthew 20:1-16:

For the kingdom of heaven is like a landowner who went out early in the morning to hire men to work in his vineyard. He agreed to pay them a denarius for the day and sent them into his vineyard.

About the third hour he went out and saw others standing in the marketplace doing nothing. He told them, "You also go and work in my vineyard, and I will pay you whatever is right." So they went.

He went out again about the sixth hour and the ninth hour and did the same thing. About the eleventh hour he went out and found still others standing around. He asked them, "Why have you been standing here all day long doing nothing?"

"Because no one has hired us."

He said to them, "You also go and work in my vineyard."

When evening came, the owner of the vineyard said to his foreman, "Call the workers and pay them their wages, beginning with the last ones hired and going on to the first."

The workers who were hired about the eleventh hour came and each received a denarius. So when those came who were hired first, they expected to receive more. But each one of them also received a denarius. When they received it, they began to grumble against the landowner. "These men who were hired last worked only one hour," they said, "and you have made them equal to us who have borne the burden of the work and the heat of the day."

But he answered one of them, "Friend, I am not being unfair to you. Didn't you agree to work for a denarius? Take your pay and go. I want to give the man who was hired last the same as I gave you. Don't I have the right to do what I want with my own money? Or are you envious because I am generous?"

So the last will be first, and the first will be last.